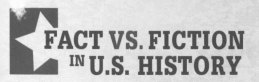

T0020173

CHRISTOPHER COLUMBUS

AND THE AMERICAS:
SEPARATING FACT FROM FICTION

by Peter Mavrikis

Consultant: Roberto Múkaro Borrero

CAPSTONE PRESS
a capstone imprint

Capstone Captivate is published by Capstone Press, an imprint of Capstone.
1710 Roe Crest Drive
North Mankato, Minnesota 56003
capstonepub.com

Library of Congress Cataloging-in-Publication Data
Names: Mavrikis, Peter, author.
Title: Christopher Columbus and the Americas : separating fact from fiction / by Peter Mavrikis.
Description: North Mankato, Minnesota : Capstone Press, a Capstone imprint, [2022] | Series: Fact vs. fiction in U.S. history | Includes bibliographical references and index. | Audience: Ages 8-11 | Audience: Grades 4-6 |
Summary: "In 1492, Christopher Columbus discovered the Americas. Or did he? Look at all the facts and discover the fiction through primary sources, infographics, and leveled text. Readers will learn the full story about Christopher Columbus's famous voyage"— Provided by publisher.
Identifiers: LCCN 2021002539 (print) | LCCN 2021002540 (ebook) | ISBN 9781496695635 (hardcover) | ISBN 9781496696731 (paperback) | ISBN 9781977154002 (eBook PDF) | ISBN 9781977155719 (kindle edition)
Subjects: LCSH: Columbus, Christopher—Juvenile literature. | Explorers—America—Biography—Juvenile literature. | Explorers—Spain—Biography—Juvenile literature. | America—Discovery and exploration—Spanish—Juvenile literature.
Classification: LCC E111 .M445 20022 (print) | LCC E111 (ebook) | DDC 970.01/5092 [B]—dc23
LC record available at https://lccn.loc.gov/2021002539
LC ebook record available at https://lccn.loc.gov/2021002540

Image Credits
Getty Images: DeAgostini, 7, 8; iStockphoto: whitemay, back cover, 12, ZU_09, 15; Library of Congress: cover (bottom), 11, 13, 28; Newscom: Album/Oronoz, 22, VWPics/Mel Longhurst, 14; The New York Public Library: cover (top right), 6; North Wind Picture Archives: 9, 17, 20, 23, 24; Raindrop Games: Artwork by Priscillia Pun from Arrival: Village Kasike, 16; Shutterstock: AnnyStudio, 10, Ben Hovland, 27, Everett Collection, 5, 21, Michael Rosskothen, cover (top left); XNR Productions: 19

Editorial Credits
Editor: Gena Chester; Designer: Heidi Thompson; Media Researcher: Svetlana Zhurkin; Production Specialist: Laura Manthe

Thank you to our consultant, Roberto Múkaro Borrero, member of the Taíno Tribal Nation

All internet sites appearing in back matter were available and accurate when this book was sent to press.

Table of Contents

Introduction... **4**

Chapter One
Proving the Earth Is Round **6**

Chapter Two
Setting Sail.. **10**

Chapter Three
Discovering the "New" World **14**

Chapter Four
A Motivated Leader **18**

Chapter Five
We Come in Peace.................................... **22**

Chapter Six
From Fame to Chains **26**

Glossary.. **30**
Read More **31**
Internet Sites.. **31**
Index.. **32**

Words in **bold** are in the glossary.

Introduction

"In fourteen hundred ninety two, Columbus sailed the ocean blue. . . ." So begins the famous poem. Some of the information in the poem is true. Historians know plenty of facts about Columbus's voyage. They know some things in the poem are fiction.

Other details were left untold. So what really happened? Did Columbus and his sailors believe that they would sail off the edge of a flat Earth? Was Columbus the first European to reach—and discover—America? Did the famous explorer die poor or successful? Read on to find out more about Columbus and the stories that have been told for the last 500 years.

Illustration from 1892 of Columbus and his crew seeing land

Fact!

Most depictions of Columbus's voyage were made hundreds of years after he set sail, and most are not historically accurate. All known portraits of Columbus himself were created after his death, so pictures of him are also likely inaccurate.

Chapter One

Proving the Earth Is Round

Columbus did sail across the Atlantic Ocean. He started his journey on August 3, 1492. The journey began in Spain where he set sail with a crew of 87 men. They sailed on three ships.

Some people think Columbus sailed to prove Earth was round. This **myth** most likely came from a book written almost 340 years after Columbus's first

expedition. Published in 1828 by American author Washington Irving, *A History of the Life and Voyages of Christopher Columbus* incorrectly states that Columbus set sail to prove that Earth was round and not flat.

Washington Irving was best known for his short stories, but he also worked as a historian and biographer.

The Edge of the World

Christopher Columbus never needed to prove that Earth was round. Like most educated people at the time, he already knew this. Sailors also knew that Earth was not flat. Although sea travel was dangerous for other reasons, including storms and shipwrecks, falling off the edge of the world was not a concern.

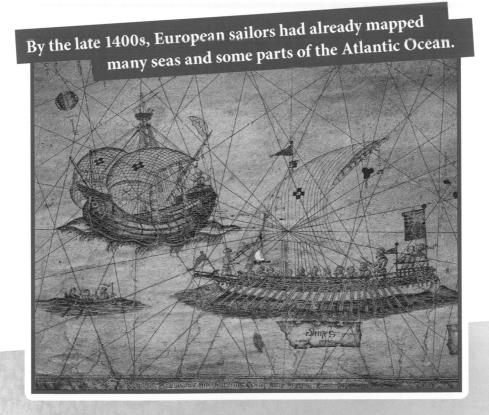

By the late 1400s, European sailors had already mapped many seas and some parts of the Atlantic Ocean.

It's a Wide, Round World!

The idea of a round Earth dates back to the ancient Greeks. Pythagoras, a Greek philosopher and mathematician, first thought of Earth as round in the sixth century BCE. Aristotle, another Greek philosopher, helped demonstrate that Earth was round by showing the curve of the **horizon**.

Illustrations during Columbus's time prove people knew Earth was round. Here, the geographer Ptolemy holds up a globe to represent Earth.

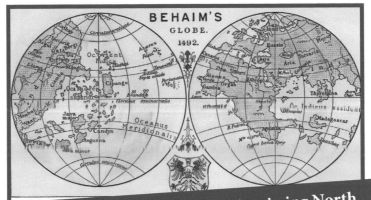

This map of the world from 1492 is missing North and South America and has other inaccuracies.

At the time, no one knew the actual **circumference** of Earth. Columbus's calculations, though, were not even as accurate as the ones the ancient Greeks made long before Columbus set sail. Columbus believed Earth was smaller than it actually is. He thought Asia was around 5,000 miles (8,000 kilometers) from Spain. But it's actually closer to 10,000 miles (16,000 km). He also never imagined the route would be blocked by two landmasses—North and South America!

Fact!

Ancient Greeks figured out that Earth was round more than 2,000 years ago. Before that, many people believed that if they reached the end of the world, they would fall off its edge and into nothingness.

Chapter Two

Setting Sail

On August 3, 1492, Christopher Columbus set sail for Asia. His mission was to find a shorter, quicker route to Asia. This sea route would open new markets. The **trade** from these markets would bring wealth to Columbus and the country that paid for his expedition. At the time, cinnamon, clove, pepper, and nutmeg were found only in Asia. The people of Europe liked these **exotic** spices and were willing to pay a lot for them.

Spices such as cinnamon and clove were highly valued and difficult for Europeans to get.

Columbus needed money to pay for his voyage. He asked the **monarchs** of England, France, and Portugal for help, but they refused. Columbus's luck changed when he went to Spain. The Spanish monarchs—King Ferdinand and Queen Isabella—agreed to pay for Columbus's expedition. They also gave him three ships.

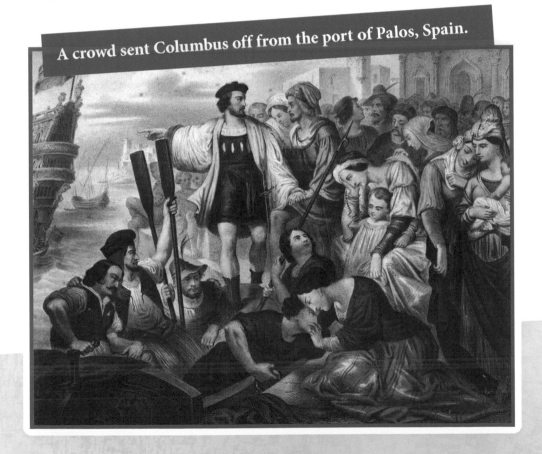

A crowd sent Columbus off from the port of Palos, Spain.

The *Santa Clara, Pinta,* and *Santa Maria*

For a very long time, schoolchildren were taught that Columbus sailed across the ocean on the *Niña*, *Pinta*, and the *Santa Maria*. The actual name of the *Niña* was the *Santa Clara*. The *Santa Maria* had many names. It was first known as *La Gallega*. The original name of the third ship, the *Pinta*, has been long forgotten.

Of Columbus's three ships, the *Santa Maria*, first known as *La Gallega*, was the largest.

At the time, it was common to name ships after Christian saints. But sometimes, these names did not stick. Columbus's crew gave the three ships nicknames. The *Santa Clara* became *La Niña*, which means "the girl." *La Pinta*, the third ship's nickname, translates to "the painted one." Columbus himself changed the name of *La Gallega* to *Santa Maria*. The crew had nicknamed the ship *Marigalante*, but Columbus liked the more religious name *Santa Maria*, or Saint Maria, better.

Fact!

A popular myth is that Queen Isabella sold the royal jewels to pay for Christopher Columbus's expedition. This is not true. Most of the money came from bankers and private investors who lived in Spain.

Isabella I, queen of Spain

Chapter Three

Discovering the "New" World

After spending 10 weeks sailing across the ocean, Columbus and his crew finally spotted land. On October 12, 1492, they stepped onto the shores of an island Columbus called San Salvador. San Salvador means "Holy Savior" in Spanish.

Visitors can learn about the everyday life and culture of Indigenous peoples in reconstructed villages. This village in Cuba is modeled after traditional villages of the Taíno people.

Even though Columbus called the island San Salvador, it already had a name. The **Indigenous** peoples living on the island called the land Guanahani. Believing that he had reached an island in Asia, Columbus called the Indigenous people "Indios," or Indians. The name referred to the Indus river valley located in South Asia. Little did Columbus know that he was nowhere near his planned destination.

Fact!

In 1501, Amerigo Vespucci was the first European explorer to recognize South America as a new landmass. Before Vespucci, other European explorers, including Columbus, believed that they had, in fact, reached Asia.

Amerigo Vespucci

The Taíno

Generations of schoolchildren have been taught that Columbus discovered a "new" world. The truth is that North and South America had already been home to millions of people for thousands of years. The Indigenous peoples Columbus first met are called the Taíno. Their traditional homelands include many Caribbean islands—present-day Cuba, Puerto Rico, Jamaica, and others. They were among the many Indigenous Nations across the continents of North and South America.

The Taíno developed a successful society with complex religious, political, and social systems.

Norse Explorers

Columbus might not have even been the first European to sail to what would become known as the Americas. There is evidence that the Norse—also known as Vikings—reached North America 500 years before Columbus. These fearsome warriors from northern Europe explored and settled Iceland and Greenland. In the year 1000 CE, many believe the Norse explorers reached land that is now part of present-day Canada.

Evidence of the Norse in North America is hard to come by. There is no written record—only stories, or sagas—that make it hard for historians to separate fiction from fact.

Chapter Four

A Motivated Leader

Before Columbus set off on his journey, he made a deal with the Spanish Crown. The deal gave him 10 percent of all the riches he found and made him governor of all the lands he claimed for Spain. But being a good governor, and treating the Indigenous peoples of those lands well, was not his priority. Instead, he was eager to find spices and gold.

As soon as Columbus landed on the shore of Guanahani, he traded with the Taíno. Columbus offered them cheap ornaments and beads of glass.

In return, the Taíno gave him cloth, colorful parrots, and small pieces of gold. To Columbus's surprise, there was no sign of the type of wealth he had expected to find.

Columbus kept searching. He set sail for other islands looking for treasure. He forced several Taíno to act as his guides. At every stop, the Indigenous people he traded with pointed to other islands where they said gold could be found. It seemed as though riches were always just out of reach.

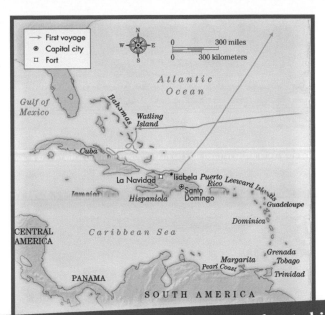

The exact location of Guanahani has been lost to history, but many believe it is present-day San Salvador, which was once known as Watling Island.

Return to Spain

In December 1492, the *Santa Maria* struck rocks in shallow Caribbean waters. The damaged ship soon sank. With the help of the local Taíno people, the crew saved what they could. They used the wood from the ship to build a fort on an island they named Hispaniola. They called their **colony** La Navidad.

Columbus spent three months searching for gold and spices—but found nothing. He left 39 of his crew at La Navidad and continued on. In January 1493, Columbus set sail back to Spain.

The *Santa Maria* sank off the coast of present-day Haiti.

A Visit to the Royal Court

Columbus arrived back in Spain on March 15, 1493. Eager to learn of his journey, King Ferdinand and Queen Isabella invited him to their court. Although Columbus did not return with the riches he had promised, he did have a lot to show—amber, exotic birds, and what little gold he had been able to collect. He also had kidnapped some Taíno people and displayed them before the royal court.

Columbus at King Ferdinand and Queen Isabella's court

The king and queen were impressed with Columbus's adventures. They agreed to pay for a second expedition. This time, Columbus set sail with 17 ships and more than 1,000 men.

WAS COLUMBUS SPANISH?

To the Spanish, Columbus was known as Cristóbal Colón. But Christopher Columbus was actually born Cristoforo Colombo in Genoa in 1451. Once an independent republic, Genoa became part of Italy more than 400 years after Columbus was born.

Christopher Columbus

Chapter Five

We Come in Peace

Columbus's voyages gave Spain access to new lands. This time of exploration became known as the Age of Discovery. For the Spanish Crown, it was an opportunity to gain wealth. King Ferdinand and Queen Isabella were also eager to **convert** the Taíno people. They wanted to spread the Catholic religion. But this is only one side of history. For the Taíno living in the Caribbean, Columbus's explorations would have a devastating effect.

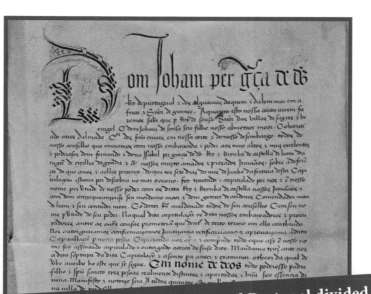

In 1494, the monarchs of Spain and Portugal divided up the Americas in the Treaty of Tordesillas.

A Time of Conflict

In late November 1493, Columbus returned to Hispaniola only to find the small settlement of La Navidad in ruins. While he was away, the Spaniards he had left behind had become violent toward the Taíno. Conflicts broke out. The fort was burned to the ground, and all 39 of Columbus's men had died.

Columbus and those he put in charge killed many Taíno to try to stop any resistance to his rule.

Forced Labor

Columbus founded a second colony. He named it La Isabela after Spain's queen. Under his deal with the king and queen, Columbus was governor of La Isabela. But instead of making peace with the Taíno people, he continued his search for gold.

Things changed quickly for the Taíno. The men Columbus brought with him on the second expedition also treated Taíno people poorly. The Spaniards forced many of them to search for gold. They also stole what gold the Taíno had. The Spaniards committed many acts of horrific violence against the Taíno. Columbus did nothing to stop it. Many Taíno were also dying of diseases brought by the Spanish.

Columbus and his men forced many Taíno to search for gold and work on Spanish farms. He and his men killed those who resisted.

Enslavement

In early 1495, Columbus enslaved 1,600 Taíno people. He sent 500 of them to Spain. Two hundred Taíno did not survive the voyage. And many others did not survive being enslaved in Spain.

The king and queen were not pleased with this decision. They wanted the Taíno to convert to Christianity, but the monarchs didn't want them to be enslaved. In 1496, Columbus himself returned to Spain and faced the monarchs.

DEADLY DISEASES

It is hard to say how many Taíno people lived on the islands when Columbus first arrived. The number could have been anywhere between 125,000 and 1 million. There are some estimates of more than that. Sadly, it is true that thousands of Taíno were killed, while many more died as a result of diseases, including smallpox, typhus, influenza, and measles. These diseases were brought by the European explorers and settlers. Sixty years after Columbus's arrival, relatively few Taíno remained throughout the Caribbean.

Chapter Six

From Fame to Chains

Christopher Columbus has been celebrated around the world. Provinces, cities, rivers, schools, and even a university and a currency—the colón in Costa Rica—are named after him. His story is one of discovery and wealth. But that story has begun to change. Through the work of Indigenous and non-indigenous **activists** and historians, people are remembering the darker side of his story—especially the brutal violence he and his men used against the Taíno people. And the reality is that Columbus never returned to Spain with great riches from his voyages.

After Columbus's second expedition, King Ferdinand and Queen Isabella began doubting his discoveries. Where were all the riches of Asia? Nothing that Columbus promised had been delivered. Columbus was given another chance, but his time was running out. On May 30, 1498, he set off on his third expedition.

Broken Promises

The Spaniards on Hispaniola were not happy to see his return. They believed Columbus was a bad governor. Many suffered, none more so than the Taíno. Columbus and a small crew went back to exploring different islands, leaving La Isabela without a governor.

After two more years of searching without success, Columbus went back to Spain. But this time, he was sent back as a prisoner. The Spaniards on Hispaniola and the Spanish Crown had had enough of his broken promises.

Because of Columbus's crimes against Indigenous peoples, some statues made to honor his memory are protested against and torn down.

The Final Voyage

Some stories say Columbus died poor and jailed in Spain. This is not true. Although Columbus did spend six weeks in prison, he was set free by King Ferdinand. The king also allowed one more trip. But Columbus could not return to the island of Hispaniola. He was no longer governor.

In May 1502, Columbus went on his fourth and final expedition. He still thought he was in Asia, but this time he was off the coast of Central America. After two years, he did not find gold or spices, and he and his crew shipwrecked in Jamaica. He survived with help from local Taíno. After seven months, he and his crew were rescued. Columbus returned to Spain for good on November 7, 1504.

Christopher Columbus

Columbus died in Spain in 1506. He had explored many lands unknown to Europeans. But in the end, he was disappointed with his failures.

Timeline

1451	Christopher Columbus is born in Genoa (today part of Italy).
August 3, 1492	Columbus and his crew set sail on the *Niña*, *Pinta*, and the *Santa Maria*.
October 12, 1492	After 10 weeks sailing across the Atlantic Ocean, Columbus spots land and soon meets Indigenous Taíno people.
December 24–25, 1492	The *Santa Maria* sinks off the coast of Hispaniola.
January 2, 1493	Columbus sets sail for Spain, bringing items from his exploration, as well as Taíno he kidnapped, to King Ferdinand and Queen Isabella.
September 25, 1493	Columbus begins his second expedition with 17 ships and more than 1,000 men.
May 30, 1498	Columbus embarks on his third expedition.
1500	Columbus is replaced as governor and returns to Spain in chains.
November 7, 1504	Columbus returns to Spain after his fourth and final expedition.
May 20, 1506	Columbus dies at age 54 in Valladolid, Spain.
1828	Washington Irving publishes *A History of the Life and Voyages of Christopher Columbus*.

Glossary

activist (AK-tih-vist)—person who works for social or political change

circumference (sir-KUHM-frehns)—the distance around something

colony (KAH-luh-nee)—a settlement under the control of the home country

convert (kuhn-VURT)—to change from one religion or faith to another

exotic (ek-ZAH-tuhk)—something that comes from a foreign land

expedition (ek-spuh-DIH-shuhn)—a journey with a goal, such as exploring or searching for something

horizon (huh-RYE-zuhn)—the line where the sky and the earth or sea seem to meet

Indigenous (in-DIH-juh-nuhs)—people native to a place before the arrival of colonizers

monarch (MAHN-ark)—a ruler of a country

myth (MITH)—a false idea that many people believe

trade (TRAYD)—the buying and selling of goods

Read More

Brink, Christopher. *Christopher Columbus: Controversial Explorer of the Americas.* New York: Cavendish Square, 2019.

Krensky, Stephen. *Christopher Columbus: Explorer and Colonist.* New York: Random House Children's Books, 2020.

Slader, Erik and Thompson, Ben. *The Age of Exploration: Totally Getting Lost.* New York: Roaring Brook Press, 2019.

Internet Sites

Christopher Columbus Facts & Worksheets
kidskonnect.com/people/christopher-columbus/

Today in History: Columbus Day
loc.gov/item/today-in-history/october-12/

United Confederation of Taíno People
uctp.org

Index

Age of Discovery, 22
Aristotle, 8
Atlantic Ocean, 6

calculations, 9

diseases, 24, 25

Earth, 4, 6, 7, 8, 9
enslavement, 25

Genoa, 21
gold, 18, 19, 20, 24, 28
governors, 18, 24, 27, 28
Guanahani, 15, 18

Hispaniola, 19, 23, 27, 28
horizon, 8

Irving, Washington, 6

King Ferdinand, 11, 20, 22, 26, 28

La Isabela, 24, 27
La Navidad, 19, 23

Norse, 17

prison, 28
Pythagoras, 8

Queen Isabella, 11, 13, 20, 22, 26

routes, 9, 10

San Salvador, 14, 15
ships, 6, 11, 12, 13, 19, 21
spices, 10, 18, 19, 28

Taíno, 16, 18, 20, 22, 23, 24, 25, 26, 27

Vespucci, Amerigo, 15
violence, 24, 26